THE PATRIARCHS

ENCOUNTERING THE GOD OF ABRAHAM, ISAAC, AND JACOB

Leader Guide

BETH MOORE

LifeWay Press®
Nashville, Tennessee

About the Author

JULIE WOODRUFF realized God's call to ministry as a college sophomore. Over the years that calling has taken the shape of youth ministry, women's ministry, writing, Bible study and conference leadership. Julie is a graduate of Louisiana College and Southwestern Baptist Theological Seminary. She is an active women's ministry leader in her church and community and began the women's ministry at West Conroe Baptist church in Conroe, Texas, where her husband was the pastor for over 13 years. Julie has written leader material and learning activities for a number of Bible-study and discipleship resources for authors T. W. Hunt, Melana Hunt Monroe, and Beth Moore. She has also written devotions for Sandi Patty's and CeCe Winans' CD releases. Julie resides in Hendersonville, Tennessee, with her husband, Sid, and their two teenagers, Jordan and Lauren.

Published by LifeWay Press®
© 2005 • Beth Moore
Second printing August 2005

ISBN 0-6331-9753-X

Dewey Decimal Classification: 222.11

Subject Headings: PATRIARCHS (BIBLE) \ GOD \ BIBLE O.T. GENESIS 12–50 \ STUDYING AND TEACHING

Atlas map © 1998 Broadman and Holman Publishers. All rights reserved.

Unless otherwise indicated, Scripture quotations are from the Holy Bible, New International Version, copyright © 1973, 1978, 1984 by International Bible Society.
Scripture quotations identified KJV are from the King James Version.
Scripture quotations identified NASB are from the New American Standard Bible © Copyright The Lockman Foundation, 1960, 1962, 1963, 1968, 1971, 1972, 1973, 1975, 1977, 1995. Used by permission.
Scripture quotations identified HCSB are from the Holman Christian Standard Bible®, copyright © 1999, 2000, 2001, 2002, 2003 by Holman Bible Publishers. Used by permission.

To order additional copies of this resource, WRITE to LifeWay Church Resources Customer Service; One LifeWay Plaza; Nashville, TN 37234-0113; FAX (615) 251-5933; ORDER ONLINE at www.lifeway.com; or VISIT the LifeWay Christian Store serving you.

Printed in the United States of America

Leadership and Adult Publishing
LifeWay Church Resources
One LifeWay Plaza
Nashville, TN 37234-0175

Contents

Facilitating a Group

1. Seek the approval of your pastor. Enlist his OK and, ideally, his blessing. Encourage him to announce this new opportunity for women. Since women fill many vital positions in the body of Christ, the deepening of their spiritual lives should be a high priority in any church.

2. Present the idea of studying *The Patriarchs* to the women of your church, and ask how many would like to be involved. You need an approximate participant number, even before the registration session, so you can order books, enlist small-group leaders, and reserve rooms.

3. Choose 11 consecutive weeks on your church calendar that will allow maximum participation. Schedule one introductory session and 10 study sessions. Fall and spring sessions tend to have the best attendance.

4. Determine from the level of interest whether to schedule sessions during the day, in the evening, or both. Try to offer a time slot that will meet the needs of women employed outside the home.

5. Try to offer childcare. This provision will increase your attendance and encourage mothers' weekly participation.

6. After approximating the participant number, order materials directly from LifeWay Church Resources Customer Service by calling 1-800-458-2772 or by visiting your local LifeWay Christian Store. Purchase one member book for each participant and one leader guide for each facilitator.

7. Enlist one facilitator or leader for each group of up to 12.

8. Once leaders have been enlisted and dates reserved on the church calendar, take advantage of whatever avenues your church offers for promoting *The Patriarchs*. This study is a wonderful opportunity for outreach. If possible, invite women from the community who are interested in a Bible-based study. Church bulletins, newsletters, handouts, posters, and word-of-mouth are excellent and inexpensive ways to advertise. Sometimes local radio stations will announce events in the community free of charge. Research to discover available promotion ideas and then take advantage of them!

9. Pray, pray, and keep praying that God will bring both the members and leaders that He desires to this Bible-based study and that He will validate the study time with His obvious presence and apparent activity!

After you have completed each of the preceding steps, you're on your way! Now it's time to prepare for registration and your introductory meeting!

Just Between Us

Because of my love for in-depth Bible study, I've tried to make it my business to know what works and what doesn't in a ladies' Bible-based study. Through the years I've asked many participants what they liked or did not like about the way their Bible studies were conducted. I've also offered countless evaluations at the conclusion of those which I have taught. I believe women are looking for the following characteristics in the administration of their group Bible studies:

- Women are very busy in our culture, and they want organization! When they give the precious resource of their personal time, it is undoubtedly at the sacrifice of something else. They want to participate in a well-planned program.
- Women who register for in-depth Bible study want the greater emphasis to remain on the Bible study. In other words, during discussion time, they are more interested in what God has to say and the response of the women to His Word than they are in haphazard opinions. The effective leader will keep discussions focused on the women's responses to God's Word.
- Women desire well-respected guidelines rather than stringent restrictions about attendance and confidentiality. An effective leader makes the group aware that if guidelines are respected, restrictions won't be needed.
- Women want to meet and feel that they are connected to other women. They want to know they are missed when they are absent and that they are valuable additions to the group when they are present.

The Patriarchs includes 10 weeks of Bible study and 11 video sessions for an 11-week group experience. Use these instructions for making your Bible study an enjoyable experience.

Leader Qualifications

You don't need a list of qualifications or years of teaching experience to lead *The Patriarchs*. You simply need an available and teachable heart prepared by God. Rather than teaching the material, you will help members learn for themselves.

Before the Session

1. Complete the activities in the member book each week.
2. Pray for each member of your group by name.
3. Pray for God's guidance in your preparation for each week's group session.
4. Carefully read through the weekly session guides, choosing plan A, plan B, or a combination of the two. Prepare for each suggested question and activity.
5. Arrange your room to meet the needs of your group. An intimate setting seems most beneficial.
6. Secure a DVD player and monitor for the large group's use during the entire study.

During the Session

1. Arrival Activity (10 min.)

- Greet each member and distribute name tags. Learn every member's name and use it when you speak to her.
- Share prayer requests, graciously reminding members to be brief and to the point!
- List requests as you receive them so that you can refer to them as you pray.
- Lead the group to pray for each request. Ask for God's presence and blessing throughout the session.

2. Review Plans for Each Session

Plan A: Review the Week's Principal Questions and Personal Discussion Questions (45 min.)

Look for brief, basic answers to the Principal Questions. Seek to confirm that the study content was received and understood. Answers should be obvious as members complete the weekly reading and learning activities; however, ahead of time, compose basic answers to the questions and use them to correct any misconceptions. Each day's Principal Question will be followed by a Personal Discussion Question. Each answer should be completed in two to three minutes.

Personal Discussion Questions can be answered by anyone who feels comfortable sharing. Do not pressure members to share personal answers, but allow them the opportunity to share. Ask them to be discreet and to never name another person who could be hurt by the discussion. Appropriate discussion of these questions is invaluable to the application of the unit. Be prepared to redirect should the discussion become inappropriate. Pray for discretion and boldness at such times.

Plan B: Guide Participants in Each Week's Suggested Activities (45 min.)

Plan B is provided for those group leaders who want a more activity-based learning experience. Get creative! Use the enrichment activities to review and reflect on the truths the Holy Spirit has illuminated for participants during their personal study. Pray and follow the Spirit's leadership. You may use as many of the suggested learning activities or as few as you determine will be best for your group. You may also use plan A and supplement with activities from plan B.

3. Conclude Session (5 min.)

- Give a brief introduction to the next week's study, and encourage members to complete their home study.
- Address any unexpected needs or comments.
- Close with prayer.
- Dismiss to the large group to view Beth's teaching on video. (Allow approximately 55 min.)

After the Session

1. While the session is fresh on your mind, record concerns expressed by group members. Pray for these concerns throughout the week.
2. Evaluate the session by asking yourself the following questions. You may want to record your answers in a journal.
   - Was I adequately prepared for today's session?
   - Did I begin and end on time? If not, how can I use the time more wisely next session?
   - Does anyone need extra encouragement this week? If so, note whether a card or a phone call is appropriate. Remember to follow up on each one.
   - What was my overall impression of the session?
3. Read the next session guide in order to prepare for the next group time.

Introductory Session

Before the Session

1. Be prepared to register members. Have member books, registration cards or sign-up sheets, pens, and name tags. Assume responsibility for new members' first impression. Make your name tag, be ready to greet members with enthusiasm, anticipate members' questions with knowledgeable answers, make participants feel welcome, and invite them to take a seat.
2. Play the music CD from the leader kit as members enter the room. If desired, have light refreshments available.
3. Pray for each group member and leader.

During the Session

1. Welcome members and introduce yourself. Ask the members to choose objects that they can use to describe themselves. (One might choose flowers because she likes to brighten someone's day; another might choose an electrical outlet because she likes to empower people.) Allow group members time to share their names, what they have chosen, and why. As the leader, give your choice first so that they will get the hang of it.
2. Pray for group members by name, asking God to open eyes, ears, and hearts to see, hear, and receive truth throughout the study. Pray that the group will have the perseverance to complete what they have started.
3. Give instructions and information about the course, including the following:
   a. Have members scan the first week's daily assignments in the member book. Explain that they are to complete a week of study before each group session. Emphasize that although the daily assignments are crucial, members should attend the weekly sessions even if their work is incomplete. Tell them to expect each daily assignment to take about 45 minutes.
   b. Encourage members to read the introduction in the member book before beginning their study.
   c. Using the introduction to week 1 as an example, explain that the format is designed to enhance learning. Point out that the Principal Questions, listed in the introduction to each week, and the Personal Discussion Questions, appearing with the symbol 🐪, highlight key points in each week's material.

d. Point out the Genealogy of Abraham on the inside front cover and the map on the inside back cover.
   e. Emphasize that the primary purposes of each week's group discussion are—
      • accountability. In-depth Bible studies are most often completed successfully in a group.
      • to underscore basic biblical truths. This will be accomplished through discussion and group learning activities which ensure that the week's content has been received and understood.
      • to personally apply the study. This will be accomplished through activities in the session.
   f. Express the need to be good stewards of each session's time. Ask participants to be prompt. Emphasize that although each person's comments are vital to the discussion, members should make them brief.
4. Announce that after today's introductory meeting, members will follow this schedule each week.
   • Welcome, prayer, and discussion (50 min.). Explain that during prayer time, members will be allowed to request prayer. Ask that requests be stated in one brief sentence so the group will have time to discuss the week's content. The prayer and discussion or activity time should last about 50 minutes.
   • A break.
   • The video of Beth's teaching (approximately 55 min.).
   • Closing assignment and prayer. Explain that you will close each session by reminding members of their at-home assignment and by having prayer.
5. Ask the group whether they would like to have light refreshments and beverages each week during this break. If so, decide how this will be done.
6. View introductory video (54:18). Explain that each video presentation will be from 53 to 59 minutes and will enhance and conclude each unit of study.
7. Share closing comments. Briefly introduce week 1. Ask members to complete week 1's homework before the next session.
6. Close by praying that members will experience God's faithfulness as never before through their study of *The Patriarchs*. Collect name tags as the group departs.

Session One ❋ *Leave Your Country*

Before the Session
1. Pray for group members.
2. Secure poster or marker board, markers, and highlighters.

PLAN A
Review the Week's Questions (45 min.).

Principal Questions
1. According to Hebrews 11:8, where did Abram think he was going?
2. What did the Lord do on behalf of "Abram's wife Sarai" (Gen. 12:17)?
3. What kind of division developed between Abram and Lot (Gen. 13:5-7)?
4. What was Abram called in Genesis 14:13?
5. Who was Melchizedek and what made him unique?

Personal Discussion Questions
1. Why should we be interested in God's promises to Abraham (Gal. 3:6-9)?
2. Have you ever felt that you followed God in obedience to a promise only to find yourself in a desert soon after your arrival? ❑ yes ❑ no If so, explain.
3. Overcrowding increases conflict, but that may not have been the only issue. What does Proverbs 13:10 consider a breeding ground for many quarrels?
4. "Faith makes us independent, but not indifferent." What do you think that means?
5. At this season in your life, what is your greatest need?

PLAN B
Preparing Enrichment Activities
1. Secure a concordance, paper, and pens or pencils.

During the Session
1. Discuss as a group the dynamics of family. How does loss affect a family? What were the family dynamics that could have affected Abram in following God?
2. Ask members to divide into triads and make a list of false gods that are worshiped today. Ask group to also list false gods that have been passed down from their ancestors. Encourage participants to discuss how those "gods" affected them, but request that they not mention any names or relationships. Reassemble the group.
3. Give each member a sheet of paper and the following assignment: "Pretend that you are Abraham and God has told you to leave and go. On the paper, describe how His instructions make you feel." Allow volunteers to share responses with the group.
4. Ask a volunteer to read Genesis 12:1-3. Ask, "What are the promises in these passages?" Have a volunteer write them on poster or marker board. Ask, "What do these promises have to do with believers?"
5. Discuss ways we can bless others. Challenge group to bless others this week.
6. Just to make sure everyone is together, trace Abram's journey on the map in the member's book. You will find this map with the journeys marked on page 32.
7. Ask the group to explain to what "Ur" (Usual Routine) can refer. Discuss why our "Urs" can be difficult to leave.
8. Ask, "What would you have done in Abraham's situation as he went down to Egypt?"
9. Share thoughts from the question on day 3, "If you were Sarai, what would the ride back to Canaan have been like?"
10. Ask, "What was the significance of Abram's going back to Bethel?" Have volunteers share testimonies about the significance of returning to a place of worship and fellowship with God.
11. Discuss Abraham and Lot's departure. Ask, "How often do we distance ourselves from God on the basis of what looks good?"
12. Compare 2 Corinthians 6:17 and Matthew 28:19-20. Ask, "How do you reconcile the apparent contradiction?"
13. Ask the group to share the names of God they listed on page 30 in the member book. If someone couldn't think of a name, have the group help to find one. Using the concordance for assistance, locate the Scripture that uses that particular name.
14. Conclude with a prayer of praise.

Conclude Session (5 min.)
1. Give a brief introduction to next week's study, and encourage members to complete their home study.
2. Close with prayer.
3. Dismiss to the large group to view Beth's teaching on session 1 video [54:17].

Session Two ❀ The Approaching and Approachable God

Before the Session

1. Pray for group members.

PLAN A

Review the Week's Questions (45 min.).

Principal Questions

1. In Genesis 16:7, God began dialogue with Hagar through questions. What were they?
2. According to Genesis 17:2, what had the Lord come to Abram to do?
3. Describe the blessings specifically spoken over Sarah's life found in Genesis 17:15-16.
4. What very specific prophecy did Sarah overhear (Gen. 18:10)?
5. How does Ephesians 4:18-19 partially explain the condition of Sodom?

Personal Discussion Questions

1. What name did Hagar give God? Is there any particular reason that name means something special to you right now?
2. The New Testament emphasizes a circumcision of the heart. Can you see any parallels for our lives?
3. Who or what do you tend to believe holds up God's full blessing to you?
4. Do you believe in miracles? Whether your answer is yes or no, please explain why.
5. Can you think of a time when "looking back" was a grievous mistake? Share as discreetly as possible.

PLAN B
Preparing Enrichment Activities

1. Pray for group members.
2. Secure two inexpensive prizes such as candy, note pads, or gift certificates to be given to the first pair that completes their list of 10 ways they've tried to help God.
3. Make sure meeting room is equipped with markers and a white board or posters for activities.
4. Check out books of name meanings to bring to the session. (If you have difficulty finding books, a number of Web sites provide this information.)

During the Session

1. Read Psalm 8. Thank God for approaching us and allowing us the privilege to approach Him.
2. Ask the participants to pair up with the person seated to their left. Their assignment is to come up with 10 ways they have tried to "help" God. The first pair to finish wins. Share some of the lists with the group. Give prizes to the winning pair.
3. Ask for volunteers to share answers to the question on page 36, "Have you ever manipulated something that you didn't get to keep?"
4. Read Genesis 16:6-15. Discuss as a group the effect that being called "slave" might have had on Hagar. Ask, "If you were Hagar, what would you be planning to do once you got back to Egypt? What 'story' would you give your relatives?"
5. Allow the group to share personal testimonies of how God sees when no one else cares to look.
6. Divide into groups of four. Assign each group one of the following characters: Abraham, Sarai, Hagar, or Ishmael. Ask each group to discuss changes or experiences that these individuals may have gone through physically, emotionally, and spiritually in the 13 years of God's silence after Ishmael's birth. After a time of discussion, ask each group to share their thoughts.
7. Ask members if they have experienced a period of silence from God and if so, to describe the experience.
8. Read Genesis 17:1 aloud. Using a white board or poster, draw a word picture of what a "perfect" (KJV) or "blameless" (NIV) or "devout" (HCSB) person would look like. Based on the word picture, ask group members to silently evaluate their own lives.
9. Give insight into the definition of "covenant" and the significance of the covenant of circumcision that God made with Abram.
10. Ask, "What was Sarai's name changed to, and what did it mean?" Ask group members to share their name meanings with the group. Just for fun, divide into pairs. Give each pair a book of names and ask them what they would like to change their name to.
11. Discuss the miracle of Sarah having a baby. Ask the group to consider the question, "What in your life seems too hard or even impossible right now?" Pause and pray for those who share.

12. On a poster board, list the shocking things that take place in Genesis 19. Ask, "How do these passages correlate with what we see in our world today?"
13. Read 2 Chronicles 7:14 aloud. Pray for brokenness and national repentance.

Conclude Session (5 min.)
1. Give a brief introduction to next week's study, and encourage members to complete their home study.
2. Close with prayer.
3. Dismiss to the large group to view session 2 video [53:54].

Session Three ❋ Triumphs and Tests

Before the Session
1. Pray for group members.

PLAN A
Review the Week's Questions (45 min.).

Principal Questions
1. In Genesis 20 you have the first of four revelations from God through dreams in the Book of Beginnings. What was the basic message of the dream?
2. What does Genesis 18:11 explicitly tell you?
3. According to Genesis 21:8-11, what caused Sarah's drastic change in temperament?
4. What did Abraham give Abimelech in Genesis 21:28,30 and why?
5. What does Abraham tell the Hittites he needs?

Personal Discussion Questions
1. Has time ever dulled the difficulty of a poor decision, lulling you into making a similar decision? What did you learn from the experience?
2. How do you think Sarah finally figured out that God had fulfilled His promise and she was expecting Isaac?
3. How does Ephesians 1:11 speak to a present challenge in your life?
4. Has someone who doesn't know Christ requested something of you because God seems to be with you?
5. Many of us have buried loved ones. Which part of this scene sparks a memory that causes you to relate?

PLAN B
Preparing Enrichment Activities
1. Secure the following items for group activities: three by five cards, pens, poster or marker board, and markers.
2. You might want to decorate for a baby shower and have refreshments for the discussion of Isaac's birth.

During the Session
1. Begin session with prayer.
2. Play "Truth or Consequences." Give each member a three by five card. Instruct them to list four statements about themselves. Three of the four statements are to be true and one false. Have volunteers share their statements, allowing group members to guess which statement is false. Then say, "This is the second time we find Abraham lying. What was his reasoning? Why is it so difficult to tell the truth in some situations?"
3. Discuss the question on page 61. Say, "Imagine God telling you to get on your knees to pray for someone you had placed in a bad position. How would your feelings affect your prayers?"
4. Ask members to answer the following questions in pairs:
   • What stressful situations or crisis have caused you or someone you know to default to old patterns of behavior?
   • What if we began attentively and repeatedly praying for the Holy Spirit to invade and renew us so richly and deeply that even our impulses were godly? Ask them to describe the differences such a change could make in their lives.
   After time has been given for discussion, allow partners to share with the group.
5. Allow group members to discuss what Abraham and Sarah may have laughed about regarding Sarah's pregnancy. Ask, "How do you think Sarah finally figured out that God had fulfilled His promise and that she was expecting Isaac?"
6. Have members share the gifts they would bring for Isaac's baby shower. After everyone has spoken, please share Beth's gift with the group: She would bring a mother's book for Sarah with questions inviting her to share thoughts, feelings, and family history. At Sarah's age, she would not live to tell all her stories to grandchildren. The record of her faith walk would be priceless.

7. Divide participants into three groups. Assign one of the following characters to each group: Abraham, Sarah, and Hagar. Each group is to read Genesis 21:8-21 and discuss the passages from their character's point of view. When adequate time has been given, allow groups to share their findings and ideas.

8. Write the definition of *hesed* (covenant kindness and loyal love) on a marker board or poster. Ask, "What does this word mean in our relationship with God?"

9. Ask, "What did Abimelech know about Abraham (v. 23)? How did that knowledge affect their relationship? What matter did Abraham bring up to Abimelech? How did the two solve the situation?"

10. Discuss as a group what Abraham's mourning might have included. Ask, "What did he desire most of all? What was the problem?"

11. Write the definitions of "alien" and "stranger" on a marker board or poster. (*Alien: foreigner or sojourner. stranger: settler, inhabitant, foreigner, emigrant*). Say, "These words described Abraham, but they also describe us as believers on earth. We learned this week that God has 'set eternity in the man's heart.' " Close in prayer, thanking God that one day we will no longer be "aliens" on earth but citizens in heaven.

Conclude Session (5 min.)

1. Give a brief introduction to next week's study, and encourage members to complete their home study.
2. Close with prayer.
3. Dismiss to the large group to view Beth's teaching on session 3 video [53:15].

Session Four ✻ *Eyes on Isaac*

Before the Session
1. Pray for group members by name. Send notes to those who may need encouragement.

PLAN A
Review the Week's Questions (45 min.).

Principal Questions
1. What sign did the servant request, according to Genesis 24:12-14?
2. In what ways do you see a typical big brother expressed in Laban's actions?
3. What blessing was spoken over Rebekah as they sent her on her way (Gen. 24:5-9)?
4. What does a comparison of Genesis 15:15 and 25:8 suggest to you?
5. What was the occasion of Isaac and Ishmael's last recorded encounter (Gen. 21:8-10)?

Personal Discussion Questions
1. How does Ephesians 1:3 relate the concept of blessing to you?
2. Describe your own Genesis 24:50 moment.
3. List several "what ifs" you would have if you were Rebekah.

4. How do you think Isaac's marriage soothed the loss of his mother?
5. Surely you've known someone blessed by God—even if in your mirror—who still focuses on the way he or she has been wronged. Without naming names, describe how this focus appears to affect his or her life.

PLAN B
Preparing Enrichment Activities
1. Provide enough candy for winning team in activity 2.
2. Make sure meeting room is equipped with a white board and markers or posters for activity 5.
3. Obtain a sheet of paper and a pen for each group member for activity 8.
4. Have a CD player and the Patriarchs CD available.
5. Copy handout 4A and cut the questions apart. Place the slips of paper in a bag.

During the Session
1. Begin the session with prayer.
2. Divide the group into two teams. Have the first group leader draw a question out of the bag, read it aloud, and encourage her team to quietly help her answer. If her team misses the question, the other team is given the opportu-

nity to earn a point. When a team answers correctly, they score a point and get to continue to answer new questions until they miss. The team with the highest score at the end wins. Give candy to the winning team.

Answers: A. Abraham; B. a Semite or Aramean woman; C. camels, ring, bracelets; D. She would respond, "Drink and I'll water your camels also."; *E. before he finished speaking; F. very beautiful, a virgin; G. Rebekah's brother; H. bowed to the ground before the Lord; I. that Rebekah stay with them for 10 days; J. taking a walk in the field; K. covered herself; L. 100 years; M. Isaac and Ishmael; N. the cave of Machpelah near Mamre or with Sarah*

3. Have a volunteer read Genesis 12:2 and another read Genesis 24:1. Ask, "How had God blessed Abraham?" Say, "Abraham's obedience resulted in God's blessings." Then ask a volunteer to share a testimony of how God blessed her life as she chose to walk in obedience.

4. Read and discuss as a group Ephesians 5:25-27. Ask, "How do these passages relate to believers today?"

5. Write the following definition on a marker board or poster. "Minimalist: one who favors restricting ... the achievement of a set of goals to a minimum." Ask, "What are some ways we practice being minimalist today in our personal lives or our church life? How did Abraham's servant perform his task with excellence and avoid being a minimalist?"

6. Ask the group to brainstorm a list of "what if" questions that Rebekah might have had about Isaac. Encourage them to discuss what Rebekah might have thought and felt on the journey to meet him.

7. Discuss as a group how Rebekah might have helped Isaac deal with the death of his mother. Ask the group to share

testimonies of how God has used people to bring love, comfort, or joy into their lives after a loss.

8. Give each person paper and a pen. Say: "We read about Abraham's faith-walk in Hebrews 11:8-19. Write out your faith walk on the paper you have been given. List ways that God has been faithful to you." Give adequate time for group members to complete this exercise. If time allows, ask for volunteers to share. Be sensitive to those who may not have a testimony of a faith walk and set up a time outside of class to meet with them to share about faith in Jesus.

9. Have group members share answers to the question on page 99 in the homework. "Should you find yourself sitting next to Abraham in heaven, what would you tell him you most appreciated about his story?"

10. Discuss as a group the time Isaac and Ishmael spent together as they buried their father. Ask for descriptions of what their time together may have been like in the best- and the worst-case scenarios.

Conclude Session (5 min.)

1. Conclude the session by playing "Follow You to Love" on the Patriarchs CD.

2. Give a brief introduction to next week's study, and encourage members to complete their home study.

3. Close with prayer.

4. Dismiss to the large group to view Beth's teaching on session 4 video [55:59].

Session Five ❈ The Heel Grabber

Before the Session

1. Pray for group members by name. Call or send a note to thank participants for their faithfulness to the study.

PLAN A

Review the Week's Questions (45 min.).

Principal Questions

1. What explanation did God give Rebekah for her difficult pregnancy (v. 23)?

2. Read Genesis 25:24-34. Note every detail that surely fueled the rivalry between Esau and Jacob.

3. How did the Lord introduce Himself to Isaac in Genesis 26:24?

4. What were Rebekah's words to Jacob in Genesis 27:8?

5. Read Hebrews 12:16. What impact does this verse have on our understanding of Esau?

Personal Discussion Questions

1. What has God given you in a way that you have no doubt who was the Giver?

2. How do you imagine words like "cooking, preparing, and seething" describe Jacob?

3. What part of the discussion on parenting spoke most clearly to you?
4. What do you consider the most stressful moment in Genesis 27:1-40?
5. How did Christ explain the evidence of true parenting from His point of view in John 8:39-41?

PLAN B
Preparing Enrichment Activities

1. Secure marker board or posters for activities.
2. Write Scriptures on three by five cards to give to small groups. (See activities 6 and 7.)
3. Optional: Bring clothes or other items that can be used in skits in activity 7.

During the Session

1. Begin with prayer.
2. Ask a volunteer to read Genesis 25:19-33. Discuss how a person typically gets from the place of receiving a divine promise to the place of its fulfillment. Ask volunteers to share personal journeys. Ask, "How did God apparently encourage Isaac's spiritual participation toward the fulfillment of the promise of heirs" (25:21)?
3. On a marker board, write "Isaac" and "Esau." Then have volunteers write descriptions of each boy under his name.
4. Describe how Isaac and Rebekah felt about their boys. Ask, "What problems did their partiality spark? What are some causes of parental partiality? How can parental partiality affect the child?"
5. Say, "In verses 22-23, we learn that Rebekah heard God's prophesy over the twins firsthand. How had Rebekah been trying to help God keep His word all Jacob's life?"

6. Divide the class into three groups. Assign each group one of the following passages to read: Genesis 26:1-11, Genesis 26:12-22, and Genesis 26:23-34. Ask each group to pick out similarities in Abraham's and Isaac's actions then report their findings to the class.
7. Divide participants into four groups by birthdays: Jan.–March, April–June, July–Sept., Oct.–Dec. Assign each group one of the following passages: Genesis 27:1-4, Genesis 27:5-17, Genesis 27:18-29, Genesis 27:30-46. After reading the verses, each group is to come up with a skit to depict the passage they have read. When the skits are completed, ask group members to share which character they could best identify with and why.
8. Discuss as a group the importance of parental blessing.
9. Share your diagram on page 123 that depicted the evolution of Esau's emotions from grief to unchecked feelings and the plans that followed.
10. Discuss as a group how thinking vengeful thoughts toward people who hurt us can be a means of consoling ourselves.
11. Ask, "How does holding a grudge affect us?"
12. Close by asking group members to examine their own hearts. Ask, "Is there a grudge that you have been holding and need to release? If so, quietly confess it to the Father." Say, "The father of lies, Satan, wants to keep you bound by the stronghold of unforgiveness." Challenge group members to release it to the Lord today.

Conclude Session (5 min.)

1. Give a brief introduction to next week's study, and encourage members to complete their home study.
2. Close with prayer.
3. Dismiss to the large group to view Beth's teaching on session 5 video [53:37].

Session Six ❋ For the Love of Jacob

Before the Session

1. Pray for group members by name.

PLAN A

Review the Week's Questions (45 min.).

Principal Questions

1. According to Genesis 29:11, what did Jacob do after removing the stone and watering the sheep?
2. What excuse did Laban offer for deceiving Jacob (v. 26)?
3. What critical emotional point did Leah reach with the birth of her fourth child (v. 35)?
4. How was Laban obviously using Jacob (v. 27)?

5. Why were Rachel and Leah immediately agreeable according to Genesis 31:14-16?

Personal Discussion Questions

1. What is your customary way of greeting someone you've just met?
2. Explain why seven years could seem like only a few days. If you have a personal example when time seemed to pass similarly, share it as your explanation.
3. How did you paraphrase the statement, "the troubled child of desperation is obsession"?
4. How have you tried to "set God up for success" or come up with a formula for blessing?
5. How did you describe what might have been going through Jacob, Leah, and Rachel's minds "when Laban overtook him, and Laban and his relatives camped there, too" (v. 25)?

PLAN B
Preparing Enrichment Activities

1. Purchase prizes for the winning team in "Family Feud."
2. Secure marker board or posters for activities.
3. Make a poster with the names of children born to Jacob. (See activity 11.)
4. Make copies of handout 6B on page 29.

During the Session

1. Have volunteers read the following Scriptures aloud: Matthew 1:22-23, Matthew 28:19-20, John 14:16-18, 2 Timothy 4:18. Begin the session by thanking God for His continual presence.
2. Divide into two teams to play "Family Feud" (handout 6A). Call up a representative from each team, then ask a question. The representative who knows the answer will take a step forward. When called on, she will give the answer to the question. If her answer is correct, her team scores a point. If her answer is wrong, the other representative gets a chance to answer. If her answer is correct, that team wins a point.

   If, however, both teams get the wrong answer, then representatives can go back to their team for help. The team that thinks they can answer the question must all raise their hands. Acknowledge the team and let them share the answer. If they answer incorrectly, the other team gets a chance.

   Points are only awarded for correct answers. Keep a record of points scored on a marker board or poster. Use the questions from handout 6A on page 28.

Answers: A. when she came to the well to water sheep; B. They had to gather all the flocks and roll the stone away from the well; C. kissed her and wept loudly; D. Jacob's uncle; E. Rachel and Leah; F. Leah; G. shapely and beautiful; H. seven years; I. He gave him Leah instead of Rachel.; J. It was not the custom to give the younger daughter before the firstborn. K. 14 years; L. Leah; M. Bilhah; N. Seven; O. Joseph; P. to send him on his way so he could return to his homeland; Q. The Lord had blessed him because of Jacob.; R. that he go through the sheep and remove every sheep that is speckled or spotted, every dark-colored sheep among the lambs, and the spotted and speckled among the female goats; S. His honesty would testify for him. If Jacob had any female goats that were not speckled or spotted, or any lambs that were not black, they would be considered stolen.; T. Three; Bonus Points (5): Describe how Jacob separated the flocks. (See Gen. 30:37-42.)

3. Discuss Genesis 29:1-14. Ask, "What happened in this passage that was particularly interesting or out of the ordinary?"
4. Pair up group members and tell them to make a list of five of the funniest things they have seen adolescent boys do to win the favor of a girl. Have them share lists with the entire group. Ask, "How did Jacob act adolescent in the scene at the well?"
5. Discuss the customary way of greeting people you've just met. Ask, "Would you greet people any differently if you realized you had a tie of some kind? If so, how?"
6. On a marker board or poster, make two columns with the titles "Leah" and "Rachel." Share descriptions of both women as found in Genesis 29:14-30. Ask, "What kind of rivalry might there have been between the sisters?"
7. As a group, discuss ways our culture emphasizes physical attractiveness. Name ways this affects little girls, teenage girls, young and mature women. Read Proverbs 30:31 to the group.
8. Discuss as a group how Laban deceived Jacob. Ask, "What might Leah have felt knowing she was not Jacob's choice?"
9. Ask group members to share their answers to the activity near the bottom of page 137. Have volunteers explain how they would have counseled Leah and Rachel if they only had a minute to advise them.
10. Write the following statement on the marker board: "The troubled child of desperation is obsession." Discuss the statement and ask if any participants are willing to share examples. Ask, "How did this statement relate to Leah?"
11. Call attention to the poster made before class with the names of the children born to Jacob. What do Leah's statements reveal about her heart? What are some ways we can manipulate someone to love us?

12. Divide into triads. Assign groups the questions in handout 6B on page 29. After adequate discussion time has been given, ask for reports to the entire group.
13. Discuss the two diagrams on page 148 of the member book. Ask, "What is the difference between the two?"

Conclude Session (5 min.)

1. Give a brief introduction to next week's study, and encourage members to complete their home study.
2. Close in prayer, asking God for strength for group members to be wise when it comes to reconciliation.
3. Dismiss to the large group to view Beth's teaching on session 6 video [56:01].

Session Seven ❋ *God of the House*

Before the Session

1. Pray for group members by name.

PLAN A

Review the Week's Questions (45 min.).

Principal Questions

1. What does Matthew 5:23-24 say about making amends?
2. What was Dinah's intention when she "went out" and what happened instead?
3. Read Genesis 35:7 carefully. How did Jacob alter his previous name for this place (Bethel) on the return visit?
4. What did Rachel name her second son (35:18)? What did Jacob name the child?
5. What was the significance of the coat Jacob gave to Joseph?

Personal Discussion Questions

1. What are your thoughts concerning any unspoken reasons why Jacob might not have wanted Esau to accompany him and his family (Gen. 33:12-14)?
2. What do you think Dinah needed from those around her once they brought her home from Shechem's house?
3. Describe the last time you allowed God the time to heal you and grow you spiritually.
4. Can you think of any reason(s) why Jacob might have insisted on changing his son's name?
5. What characteristics bring out your partialities?

PLAN B
Preparing Enrichment Activities

1. Secure CD player and CD for activity 1.
2. Make copies of handouts 7A and 7B for activities 3 and 4.
3. Secure marker board or posters and markers.

During the Session

1. Begin by asking group members to share names of God that describe who He has been to them this past week (for example, My Rock, My Shepherd). Play "God of My Praise" from The Patriarchs music CD.
2. Ask, "What had happened to Jacob before he saw Esau? How did it affect him?" Ask volunteers to share testimonies (without naming names), of times they have been wounded in their encounters with God while the "Esaus" continued to run in endless confidence and vitality. Ask, "What lessons were learned? How did you grow?"
3. Divide members into three groups and assign copies of handout 7A. Allow groups time to work through the questions and report to the larger group.
4. Beth gave permission for women who find the issue of rape too difficult not to do the lesson about Dinah. Please feel free to adjust or delete any activity that you think would cause distress to someone in the group.

   Give each of the three groups a case study from handout 7B. Ask them to discuss ways believers could respond.

   Optional (instead of or with the case studies): Ask, "What disturbs you most about the rape of Dinah? What does this all-too-modern story bring to mind for you? What cruelties in our world bother you most? How can you as a believer minister to, support, and encourage those who have been through similar situations?"
5. As a group, develop a checklist of actions that can help you discern when cracks of compromise may be developing within the rock of your homes and lives.
6. On a marker board or poster, list the contrast between Rachel's and Isaac's death. Ask volunteers to share their experiences with death and dying. Ask, "Which death apparently affected Jacob more?"

7. Discuss as a group why you think Jacob changed the name of his son from Ben-oni to Benjamin. Ask, "What are some circumstances that can deeply and negatively impact a newborn's identity?"

8. Ask a volunteer to read Genesis 37:1-11. On a marker board or poster, describe each person or group listed in these verses.

9. Divide participants into 2 groups. Ask each group to come up with a modern day version of Joseph's story in skit form. After adequate preparation time has been given, allow each group to share their results.

10. As a group, consider the question, "Why do you think God might not want us to share every ounce of vision He has instilled in us?" Share examples of how Exaltation + Ego = Extravagant Humbling (member book, p. 170).

11. Close by pairing participants as "prayer partners." Instruct them to share prayer requests with one another and pray for one another throughout the week.

Conclude Session (5 min.)

1. Give a brief introduction to next week's study, and encourage members to complete their home study.

2. Close with prayer.

3. Dismiss to the large group to view Beth's teaching on session 7 video [55:04].

Session Eight ✵ Dreams and Disappointments

Before the Session
1. Pray for group members by name.

PLAN A
Review the Week's Questions (45 min.).

Principal Questions
1. What sentence did Judah pass on the woman he thought was a prostitute (v. 24)?
2. Read Genesis 39:8-9. What were Jospeh's reasons for refusing Potiphar's wife?
3. What very pointed requests did Joseph make of the cupbearer?
4. Read Genesis 41:1-13. What significance did cows have in ancient Egypt?
5. How did Joseph respond to Pharaoh's claim in Genesis 41:15, "I have heard ... when you hear a dream you can interpret it"?

Personal Discussion Questions
1. In what specific ways is God changing you as a result of the last eight weeks in His Word?
2. How could beauty be a burden?
3. When was the last time you had a dream that stuck with you and you wondered if it meant something?
4. What is something you forgot until someone was already injured by your oversight?
5. Can you relate to a long wait with a quick ending?

PLAN B
Preparing Enrichment Activities
1. Make copies of handouts 8A and 8B.
2. Secure three by five cards—enough for two cards for each participant. (See activities 4 and 13.)
3. Secure a marker board or posters and markers.

During the Session
1. Begin by asking for brief prayer requests. Ask volunteers to pray for each concern.
2. Ask a volunteer to read Genesis 38:1-11, then discuss the following.
   - Why is the sudden attention to Judah and Tamar inserted here in the Genesis narrative?
   - What was the duty of Er, Onan, and Judah himself to Tamar?
   - What did they do that made the Lord angry?
   - Why was it wrong for Judah to refuse his son's marriage to Tamar?
3. Divide the class into pairs. Ask, "What situations, if any, would ever justify wrong acts to achieve something right?" Ask volunteers to support their answer in Genesis 38 and share their findings with the group.
4. Give members a three by five card and ask them to describe the ideal job or career. You may ask, "What would you like to do? Would you like to work for someone or own your own business? What hours would you like to work? What would be the ideal geographic location?" After giving them

a few moments to think and write, ask members to share their ideal job situations with the entire group.

5. Basing your discussion on Genesis 39:1-6, ask, "In what kind of job situation did Joseph find himself? What do you see as Joseph's most important asset? What problem arose? How did Joseph handle the situation with integrity? What was the consequence of his actions?"

6. Divide the class into triads. Discuss how Joseph was able to resist Potiphar's wife. Ask each group to make a list of ways that Joseph's example could help us resist temptation in general and sexual temptation in particular. Have them share their answers with the class.

7. Give copies of handout 8A to group members. Give them time to respond, and then ask them to share their insights.

8. Ask volunteers to share the strangest dreams they have ever had. Then describe the dreams of the cupbearer and the chief baker in Genesis 40. Ask, "How did Joseph interpret the dreams? What was Joseph's one request of the cupbearer? How did the cupbearer respond?"

9. Ask participants to discuss how they would have felt had they been Joseph—forgotten in prison, hope for release gone, secure in their role as the interpreter of dreams. Ask, "What would you think of your own God-given dreams (Gen. 37:5-11)?"

10. Ask, "How long did Joseph's prison term last?" On a marker board or poster, list different emotions that Joseph must have felt during that time. Ask volunteers to

share about waiting periods in their lives and the emotions they experienced.

11. Have someone describe Pharaoh's two dreams in Genesis 41. Ask, "How did Joseph end up being the one to interpret the dream? Whom did Joseph give credit for the dream's interpretation?"

12. Give out copies of handout 8B and ask group members to answer the questions.

13. Write Luke 18:27 on the marker board or poster. "Jesus replied, 'What is impossible with men is possible with God.'" Give three by five cards to each group member, asking them to write the verse on the card. Encourage group members to memorize and claim this verse.

14. Close in prayer, asking God to help us to believe that all things are possible through Him.

Conclude Session (5 min.)

1. Give a brief introduction to next week's study, and encourage members to complete their home study.

2. Close with prayer.

3. Dismiss to the large group to view Beth's teaching on session 8 video [58:24].

Session Nine ❋ A Fragile Band of Brothers

Before the Session
1. Pray for group members by name.

PLAN A
Review the Week's Questions (45 min.).

Principal Questions
1. According to Genesis 41:50-57, what did Joseph name each of his two sons and why?
2. How did Jacob react to his sons' insistence on taking Benjamin back to Egypt (Gen. 42:38)?
3. What primary conflict is depicted in Genesis 43:1-15?
4. What did the brothers think the vizier (Joseph) was going to do to them (Gen. 43:18)?

5. Never dreaming that the cup is in their possession, what oath did the brothers make in Genesis 44:9?

Personal Discussion Questions
1. Who or what did you believe would cause you to "forget" something painful from your past? Did it work? And if so, did it last?
2. Have you ever wised up to a repeated pattern in your own relationships? If so, how has God helped you break that pattern?
3. How does guilt make you feel?
4. What reassurance does Psalm 103:10 provide?
5. Look at Genesis 45:1. Judah's words were obviously more than Joseph could stand. What do you think moved Joseph most?

PLAN B
Preparing Enrichment Activities
1. Make copies of and cut apart handout 9A, page 31.
2. Secure marker board or posters and markers.

During the Session
1. Have the class stand in a circle. Ask each person to grab the hands of two people who are not standing next to them, thus creating a tangle of arms. After everyone has two hands, tell the group to work together to untangle their knot without letting go of anyone's hand. Say, "Joseph's family was a tangled mess just like our knot. This week we begin to see the mess becoming untangled."
2. Ask for prayer requests and have group members pray silently for the person on their right.
3. Ask, "What were the names of Joseph's two sons? What did their names mean?" Write the names and meanings on a marker board or poster. Discuss the question, "Who or what did you really believe would cause you to 'forget' something painful from your past? Did it work? And if so, did it last?" Ask volunteers to share if they've had an Ephraim in their life. Ask, "Have you cooperated with God hard enough to see Him make you doubly fruitful in the very place you've known suffering or affliction?"
4. Divide members into three groups and give each group one of the three sets of events from Genesis 42 (handout 9A). Ask members to number the events in chronological order.
   After the groups have had time to complete their assignment, call for reports. Go over the list to make sure everyone has events in order and to gain an overview of Genesis 42.
5. Ask, "Imagining you are Joseph, what might you feel upon hearing your brothers say, 'The youngest is now with our father, and one is no more.' What kinds of things would go through your mind as you were described as 'no more' "?
6. Ask, "Do you think by forcing the brothers to endure all the things they had forced him to endure, Joseph was primarily seeking revenge or repentance? Explain." Plan A 2 Prin. Q
7. Divide participants into two groups. Say, "Pretend you are making a movie out of Genesis 43. What would you name it? Describe the scenes you would shoot close up with sound effects and music. Is there an emotional peak?

Is this a tear-jerker? An adventure story? A family movie? Be sure to deal with the guilt and other emotions from the various characters." Give time for groups to work, then have them share their movie ideas with the entire group.
8. Divide the class into pairs. Write the following questions on a tear sheet or poster, then ask the pairs to discuss.
   • Have you ever lost or misplaced something valuable?
   • Did you ever find it? If not, did you replace it?
   • What did the loss cost you?
   • How did finding the silver cup in Benjamin's bag affect them all?
9. Discuss how Judah took the lead in Genesis 44. Ask, "What did he say to Joseph? Does anything about Judah's plea move you personally? If so, what and why? What does this tell you about how Judah has matured? How does Judah's compelling speech bring Joseph to the breaking point?"
10. Close by asking each person to examine her own heart. Ask, "Have you given someone the chance to prove themselves or be reconciled? Have you ever had the opportunity to forgive? What did you do with your opportunity? Are you holding out hope for reconciliation with someone now? How does this story give you hope?"

Conclude Session (5 min.)
1. Pray that God will strengthen the group to do what is necessary to reconcile any broken relationships.
2. Give a brief introduction to next week's study.
3. Thank members who have been faithful to complete their home study.
4. Dismiss to the large group to view Beth's teaching on session 9 video [57:31].

Session Ten ❋ Epic Endings to the Beginning

Before the Session

1. Pray for group members by name.

PLAN A

Review the Week's Questions (45 min.).

Principal Questions

1. Read Genesis 46:1-7. What reassurances did God give Jacob about going to Egypt?
2. How did Jacob describe his years in Genesis 47:9?
3. What did Jacob do in Genesis 48:14 that displeased Joseph?
4. What are a few things our future holds for us corporately as believers in Christ?
5. Based on Jacob's words in 49:29-32, what kinds of things do you imagine preoccupied Jacob's thoughts near the end?

Personal Discussion Questions

1. God reserves the sovereign right to direct one of His children on a path He may have forbidden to another. Have you learned this lesson through personal experience?
2. How has your life seemed like a journey or a pilgrimage?
3. Think back on your history with God. What has He told you that you expect to remember with crystal clarity the rest of your life and why was it so important?
4. Can you describe a blessing of restriction in your own life?
5. Why was Jacob's reasoning about his burial important to our understanding of Genesis?

PLAN B
Preparing Enrichment Activities

1. Secure marker board or posters and markers.
2. Obtain enough three by five cards for group members to each have one for activity 9.
3. Be prepared to give an overview of Genesis 47. Read activity 4 and answer the questions.
4. Write questions for activity 2.

During the Session

1. Begin with prayer, thanking God for the opportunity to meet together throughout this study.
2. Divide participants into triads. Write the following questions on a marker board or poster, asking group members to brainstorm answers.

- If you could pick anywhere in the world to live, where would it be? Why?
- What would you miss most about leaving home?
- If you knew ahead of time that you would never return home, would you still leave?

After groups have had a few minutes to discuss, ask group members to share their responses. Write locations on the board and vote for the most exciting place.

3. Ask a volunteer to read Genesis 46:1-7. Ask, "What threads of generational connectedness do you see in this segment? What reassurances did God give Jacob about going to Egypt?" Ask a volunteer to read Genesis 46:28-30, then discuss what emotions Jacob and Joseph might have experienced as they awaited their reunion.
4. Give an overview of Genesis 47. Ask, "What reforms did Joseph set up in dealing with the famine? How did they affect the people? What did you learn about Jacob's character in this chapter?"
5. Ask group members to pair up and discuss the following.
   - Share a favorite memory about your grandparents or a senior adult who has been a good influence to you.
   - Where do you fit in the "pecking order" in your family?
   - Did you receive any "privileges of rank" as a child? If so, what were they?
   Return to large group.
6. Write *Abraham, Isaac,* and *Jacob* on a marker board or poster. Below each name, write the name of their first-born son and then the name of the son who received the blessing. Ask, "What pattern do you see? What does this pattern say about how God chooses his servants? What irony do you see in the way Jacob blesses Ephraim and Manasseh? What blessings did both sons receive? What was the only difference?" (49:19)
7. Divide the class into four small groups by numbering them off 1, 2, 3, 4. Assign each group three of Jacob's sons. Ask them to share together the symbol that represents the name, the blessing each received, and the prophecy concerning their unique destinies within their common destiny as a nation. Have them share their answers with the large group.
8. Ask, "Which two sons received the most elaborate blessings? Why do you think their blessings were more prominent? Which seem more like 'anti-blessings'?

9. Hand out three by five cards and ask group members to write out blessings they would like to pass down to the next generation. Say, "If you have children, write a blessing specifically for them. If you do not have children, write a blessing for someone who is close to you."

10. Discuss as a group why it was so important to Jacob that he be buried in Canaan. Ask, "What impact did Jacob's death have on Joseph, his family, the Egyptians, and Pharaoh's court" (see Gen. 50:1-14)?

Conclude Session (5 min.)

1. Close by asking group members to take turns sharing how other group members have blessed their lives, then pray a prayer of blessing over the group.

2. Thank members who have been faithful to complete their home study.

3. Dismiss to the large group to view Beth's teaching on session 10 video [58:36].

Viewer Guide Answer Key

Introductory Session
nation
1. Come let us; n-b-l; l-b-n; unbrick, brick
2. name; revere, reach; unspeakable, Name
3. Jews; Hebrews; children, Israel, Israelites; Judah, Judea, Judah-ites, Judah-ism, Jews
4. history, individuals

Session One
1. patriarch, prophet
2. uses, battle fear; let, win
3. score, mark, tally
4. believed, credited, righteousness; first mention, believe; [your name] believed God; esteem; act, believe, acting
5. cut, off; acceptable sacrifices, law; swear, greater, Himself; foreign attack; cross over

Session Two
1. speaking, Himself, Abraham; actions, thoughts; prophet
2. engage dialogue; cast Himself, role, man, mankind; form, shape
3. with Him; like Him
4. God, Abraham, Abraham, God; God's friend
5. here, now, then, there

Session Three
1. tests, names; prove; quality, stressful circumstances; teacher, Yah
2. hardest, dearest loves; delight; vehement, mind, tenderness, possess, presence
3. powerless; How, up, us; entreaty, staggering, rational, understanding; Here, am
4. Obedience; Keeping, faith
5. harder, test, further; preached, portrayed; Lord, provide; to see; sees; seen

Session Four
biblical, political; holy war; Arabian, Bedouins; Africa
1. insecurity, blessed, blessing, do not have; inheritor, promise; Isaac, Ishmael
2. hostility; brothers; they, their brothers; he, they; descendants, be like; becoming, descendants, be; blasphemous, son; crucified; train, blood, Crusades; Loving, stereotypes; all nations, blessed; win, love, security

Session Five

happen upon; strikes upon; randomness

1. randomly, scheduled venue, awesome encounter
2. God, Abraham, Isaac, his God
3. connection, access; gate, heaven; Israel; stone, chosen, cornerstone; build; descendants
4. increase, awareness, presence
5. set up, pillar; idols, symbols; House, Nothingness
6. top, stone; annointing; head; oil, head; priests, kings, gate; Anointed

Session Six

cover, face; face; face, him; my face; ahead, face; terrified, face; face, God; dread, someone, honestly face

1. honest appraisal; let alone; who, are, gang, game
2. honest fight; make, quit; face up, fight honestly; night, whom, struggling, light; invites, overcomers; against, for
3. honest blessing; deceiver, cheater; do not; blessing comes
4. honest name; define, how; blessing, redefined

Session Seven

keep, dreams, ourselves; exaltation, never, man; glorification, edification

Segment One

shalom; underestimated, partiality

Segment Two

A. safer, brothers
B. approval, respect, mercy, apology, appreciation, welfare

Segment Three

A. distance, close; grudge; held in, entangled, subject
B. corporately, individually; skinning; sacrifice

Segment Four

A. deliverance, before, pit
B. goat, deceived, deceived; evil; Torn, torn
C. underestimated, prejudice

Session Eight

1. strategically, representatives, influence
2. gift, skill, service, business, education; spirit, God; hovered, watery mass; Discernment; perceive, pay attention, intelligent; good, evil; pay attention; jumping, conclusions; Wisdom; clever, skillful
3. makes, take, opportunity
4. authority, submit; faithful, few, charge, many
5. high position, low position

6. harvest years, leisure years; potential; realization, action, dreamer

Session Nine

Segment One

A. moments, family; understand
B. confidence, transparent, covering

Segment Two

A. framed, picture, sovereignty; hope, healing
B. distress, anger, rival, ourselves; grieve, afflict, mental, discomfort; kindled; zealously; ignited
C. pain; deliverance; imprison
D. refuse; deliverance; destitute

Segment Three

restoring; relationships; emotions; time; resurfacing; dialogue; end; alienation

Segment Four

A. forgiveness, word; action
B. ignite, feud, skeleton, closet

Segment Five

numb, believe; frozen, numbed, inability, function

Final Point

anointing, faith, feeling

Session Ten

Eternal God, inclusions; conclusions; tie, up; ties, in

1. tied, harm, benefit, deliverance
2. tied, promise, Abraham, exodus; take notice; taken note; coffin, ark, ark, Covenant; detour, all, well
3. tied, present, future
4. ties, fulfillment, promises, ours
5. ties, unrest, longing

Retreat Guide

The Patriarchs explores important concepts such as blessing, covenant, and promise and how they forever shaped the lives of Abraham and his descendents. This retreat guide offers suggestions for conducting a retreat to launch the study.

As you plan a retreat, pray over every detail and decision. Make any adjustments needed to fit your particular situation.

ENLISTING LEADERS

Involving people in the planning increases interest and involvement, so enlist a coordinator for each major planning area. Each coordinator may need a committee to support her assignments. Conduct regular planning meetings to make sure everyone is on task, and you will greatly improve the likelihood of a successful retreat.

For smaller churches, you may choose to combine responsibilities. Remember, the point is to get as many women involved as possible so they will feel ownership of the retreat and study.

Prayer Coordinator

Prayer will be your most important tool in retreat preparation. Pray for God to lead you in all details concerning the retreat and for those who will participate in it.
1. Choose a committee of persons committed to praying.
2. Before the retreat, pray for the planning details and each coordinator by name.
3. Set up a chain of prayer warriors using women who will not attend. Ask each to sign up to pray for 15-minute increments throughout the retreat.
4. Equip the prayer warriors with specific prayer needs and the names of all participants and leaders.

Retreat Coordinator/Leader

1. Decide on the dates and location for the retreat. Possible settings are a retreat center, camp, lodge, or any location away from everyday distractions.
2. Choose and enlist small-group facilitators (preferably those who will lead small groups during the study) and committee members who can fulfill their duties with servant hearts.
3. Plan regular meetings with coordinators to discuss plans and get updates on how each committee is progressing.

Work with the Administration Coordinator to determine a schedule for the retreat.
4. Be available to all coordinators to help them accomplish their tasks and to encourage them along the way.
5. Once registration has been completed, work with the Small Group Coordinator to divide participants into nine small groups. (Spend time praying for leadership from the Holy Spirit in making these assignments.) These same small groups can meet together during the study.

If new persons join the study who didn't attend the retreat, either place them in a group or form a new one. Any new participants should view the Introductory Video before beginning the study.
6. Pray for all facilitators and participants.
7. Help other facilitators when they need assistance.
8. Speak and lead at the retreat as needed.
9. View the Introductory Video ahead of time so that you will be prepared to lead the closing invitation.

Music Coordinator

1. Provide music that exalts the Savior and invites worship during each large-group session.
2. The Patriarchs music CD is found in the leader kit and is a wonderful tool to use in planning the music.
3. Enlist musicians.
4. Make arrangements for sound equipment and desired PowerPoint® visuals. Be certain that items such as choruses, lyrics, and announcements can be easily read when they are projected.

Administration Coordinator

1. Work with the Retreat Coordinator to determine location and fee. Keep in mind the food and site expenses, as well as the schedule for the retreat.
2. Record all planning/meeting decisions.
3. Keep account of finances.
4. Work with the Promotion Coordinator to conduct registration.
5. Order a copy of *The Patriarchs* workbook for each participant. Include its cost in the total retreat cost.

6. Order the Leader Kit with DVDs. The Introductory Video will be shown at your first retreat session.
7. Arrange for access to a DVD player and large monitor.

Small-Group Coordinator

1. Assist the retreat coordinator in placing each participant in a small group of 6 to 10. These groups will form the small groups for the study. You may add persons who do not attend the retreat to small groups.
2. Encourage and pray for small-group facilitators.
3. Lead a time of orientation for facilitators. Discuss with them the key concepts of covenant and blessing and how facilitators might best lead their groups.
4. Number each group and write their number on the back of each name tag. During the opening get-acquainted celebration on Friday evening, instruct each participant to check the back of her name tag for her group number.
5. Make sure facilitators have supplies for small groups, including copies of the Name Game, poster or marker board and markers, group covenants, blessing cards, pens, paper, or anything else the facilitator may need.
6. Assign places for small groups to meet. Make signs to designate which group meets where.
7. Be available for facilitators throughout the retreat.
8. Write out a three by five blessing card for each participant's blessing envelope. You may choose to write out a comforting Scripture verse.

Decoration Coordinator

Use your creativity to make the retreat atmosphere warm and inviting. Consider these suggestions with those of your own.

1. Prepare name tags in the shape of camels (see p. 28).
2. Make goodie bags or packets for each participant. Include the schedule for the weekend, *The Patriarchs* workbook, blessing cards, and other items such as a pens, paper, fruit, candy, tissues, and so forth.
3. Watch the Introductory Video and get ideas for decorating the stage. Yours need not be elaborate.
4. Decorate tables by placing sand or hay in the middle of each one. Make three camels using artwork provided. On the first camel write Promise, on the second write Covenant, and on the third write Blessing. Tie the three camels together using raffia, then place them on the sand or hay. Or make a tent out of a paper bag folded over and write the words Promise, Blessing, and Covenant with the definitions on the tents.

5. Place placards on the walls around the room with the following names of God printed on them along with the Scripture reference.
   - LORD (Gen. 12:7)
   - Creator God, Universal Creator, Elohiym (Gen. 1:4)
   - God Most High—El Elyon (Gen. 14:18)
   - Creator of Heaven and Earth/Possessor of Heaven and Earth (Gen. 14:19,22)
   - Sovereign LORD (Gen. 15:2)
   - The God Who Sees Me—El Roi (Gen. 16:13)
   - LORD God—Covenant Maker and Keeper in relationship to man, YHWH (Gen. 2:4)
   - Lord—Master—Adhon/Adonay (Ps. 8:1)
   - Eternal God, El Olam (Gen. 21:33)
   - God Almighty—El Shaddai (Gen. 17:1; Ex. 6:3)
   - The LORD of Every Provision or "Yahweh Will Provide"—Jehovah Jireh (Gen. 22:14)
   - God of the house of God—El Bethel (Gen. 35:6-7)
   - The God—Ha Elohim (Gen. 41:25,28,32)
   - The Name—Ha Shem (2 Sam. 6:1-2)
   - The Lord, the God of your fathers—the God of Abraham, the God of Isaac and the God of Jacob (Ex. 3:15)
   - Jesus, the Lion of the Tribe of Judah (Gen. 49:9-10; Rev. 5:5)

6. People love door prizes! Try to secure some give-aways. Suggestions include a free manicure, books, stationery, or a gift certificate to a popular restaurant. Give door prizes at different times during the retreat.

Promotion/Games Coordinator

1. Promote the retreat with brochures, signs, and announcements providing all necessary information. A promotional video segment in the kit can be used to advertise the study and can be included in the retreat promotion.
2. Work with the Administration Coordinator to conduct registration. Send a letter to all participants about the retreat. Include directions to the retreat location, time the retreat will begin, and items to bring.

   Set up a registration table at the retreat location before participants arrive. Give them goodie bags, name tags, and *The Patriarchs* workbook.
3. Plan an icebreaker for Friday evening so participants can get to know one another.

Food Organizer/Hostess

1. Organize and provide all food and serving items if food is not already provided at the retreat location.
2. Plan and provide snacks for breaks. One suggestion is to ask attendees to bring a snack and a liter drink. Then you can put all snacks in a room and share.

Materials Coordinator

1. Make plenty of three by five blessing cards with camel artwork or Numbers 6:24 printed at the bottom.
2. Procure one manila envelope for each participant. Write each attendee's name on an envelope, and tape the envelopes around the walls of the meeting room.
3. Provide facilitators with materials they need for small-group sessions.

Retreat Schedule
FRIDAY EVENING
Dinner

Session 1—Promise

1. Have upbeat music playing as participants enter the room.
2. Retreat Coordinator/Leader welcomes participants.
3. Make introductions and give necessary instructions for the weekend.
4. Explain that blessing cards have been included in the member packets. Ask participants to write notes of blessing to members of their small group or anyone else. Before leaving the retreat, each person will receive her personal blessing envelope. (You'll want to make sure that each participant receives at least three blessing cards.)
5. Ask everyone to find the number on the back of the name tags. Group all those with like numbers together. These will be the small groups for the weekend as well as the study. Give each participant a copy of the Name Game, page 25. Spend time in small groups sharing your answers. Reassemble in the main meeting room for worship.
6. Retreat Coordinator/Leader explains that this evening is set aside to lift up the name of the Lord and claim His promises. Read Isaiah 26:8: "Yes, LORD, walking in the way of your laws, we wait for you; your name and renown are the desire of our hearts." Lead the group in prayer.
7. Music Coordinator leads participants in worship. Ask volunteers to read passages that describe the different names of God. Assign passages that are on the placards

around the room. For greater impact, intersperse their readings throughout the time of worship. Save *Jesus, the Lion of Judah* until the end.

Another option is to use Romans 4:13-25 to apply the promises not only to Abraham, but also to New Testament believers today.

8. View the introductory DVD of *The Patriarchs*. (54:18)
9. Read Genesis 49:9-10 and Revelation 5:5.
10. Read aloud either Genesis 15:5 or Genesis 22:17-18. Play *Jesus, The Lion of Judah*. If it's a clear, pleasant evening, you may wish to encourage everyone to spend time in prayer and worship under the stars.

SATURDAY MORNING
Breakfast

Session 2—Covenant

1. Personal Devotion Time using the devotion and poem "Trust Me with Your Isaac" (pp. 26-27).
2. Meet with the large group for a time of celebration led by the Music Coordinator. Arrange ahead of time for someone to share a testimony of God's faithfulness.
3. Divide into small groups.
4. Discuss answers to questions in today's devotion.
5. Write the following definition of covenant on a poster or marker board: "Covenant—*beriyth*—A treaty, alliance of friendship, a pledge, an obligation between a monarch and his subjects, a constitution. It was a contract which was accompanied by signs, sacrifices, and a solemn oath which sealed the relationship with promises of blessing for obedience and curses for disobedience."
6. Small group facilitator discusses the definition and importance of God's covenant with Abraham found in Genesis 15:7; 17:2. Ask, "Did God remain faithful to the covenant He made with Abraham?"
7. Ask group members what covenants they have made. Ask, "Why is a covenant so serious?"
8. Give each participant a copy of the group covenant (p. 25). Ask them to sign the covenant, making a pledge to the group that they will be faithful to God and the rest of the group for the 10 weeks of study. Have all participants sign each covenant. Stress the fact that in signing the covenant, members are committing to the Lord and one another for the duration of the study.

9. After everyone signs the covenant, the facilitator gives details concerning the date and location of the first group meeting.
10. Answer any questions group members may have.
11. Close in prayer, asking God to help group members keep the covenant they have made.

Break

Session 3—Blessing (Begin in Large Group)

1. Give each participant a sheet of paper and pen when she enters the room.
2. Music Coordinator leads group in a time of worship concentrating on God's blessings.
3. As a part of worship, at a pre-designated time, ask participants to make a list of God's blessings to them. Give them a few moments to make a list and then allow participants to share blessings. Sharing can be done all at once or a few at a time with music in between.
4. Retreat Leader discusses the concept of blessing in Scripture. The following verses from Genesis speak of blessing: 12:2; 22:17; 27:19-38; 28:3-4; 39:5; 48:1-49.
5. Project a PowerPoint® slide with the definition of "blessing." "Blessing—*Barak*; to bend the knee, to kneel down; to bless, praise; to be blessed; to pray to, to invoke, to ask a blessing; to greet."

6. Share the importance of blessing God and others. Point out that so often when we pray, we ask God to bless us. Ask, "But what are some ways that we can bless God?" Have volunteers share their ideas.
7. Divide into small groups around the room. Facilitator asks for volunteers to share with their small group blessings they may have received from family members and/or blessings they want to pass down to their family. (We will learn in our study that Jacob took Joseph's sons as his own.) Encourage single or childless women in each group to choose someone else's children to bless.
8. Pass out 3 three by five blessing cards to each of the participants and ask them to write blessings for three of their group members. If time allows, they may write a blessing to anyone else. Place cards in the envelopes provided for each group member. (Make sure to add your own pre-written blessing cards.)
9. The Music Coordinator leads the group in singing.
10. The Retreat Coordinator/ Leader speaks this final blessing over the participants as they prepare to leave: "The Lord bless you and protect you; the Lord make His face shine on you, and be gracious to you; the Lord look with favor on you and give you peace" (Num. 6:24-26).

The Name Game

Your name says a lot about you. Write your first and last name vertically in the spaces below, beginning with the first letter of your first name and ending with the last letter of your last name. Then choose a word from each category that begins with those letters. Take turns telling your group your name and the words you chose.

____ One of my favorite foods that begins with this letter is:

____ One thing I do for fun that starts with this letter is:

____ A quality about my work habits that starts with this letter:

____ A place I've been that begins with this letter is:

____ A friend or acquaintance whose first name starts with this letter is:

____ A plant or animal I like that starts with this letter is:

____ A sports or entertainment celebrity I admire whose name starts with this letter is:

____ A positive quality about me that comes out in my friendships that starts with this letter is:

____ A book or magazine I have enjoyed that begins with this letter is:

____ Something I would rather not do in my spare time that starts with this letter is:

____ A favorite possession that starts with this letter is:

____ A word that best describes my sense of humor that begins with this letter is:

____ A physical feature about myself that I especially like that starts with this letter is:

____ A place I would never want to visit on a vacation that begins with this letter is:

____ A movie or television show I enjoy that starts with this letter is:

____ A store or company that I enjoy patronizing that begins with this letter is:

Steve Sheeley, *Jump Starts and Soft Landings: 101 More Ways to Kick-Off and End Meetings* (Nashville: Serendipity House, 1998), 25.

Group Covenant

Because of God's faithfulness and with God's help, I,

_____,

covenant with my small group over the next 10 weeks to do the following:

1. Be faithful to complete what I have started, the study of *The Patriarchs*.

2. Prepare myself for small group meetings by completing my home study.

3. Attend small group meetings unless providentially hindered.

4. Pray regularly for my group leader and other members of my small group.

5. Participate openly and honestly in the group sessions.

6. Keep confidential any personal matters shared by others in the group.

7. Support and minister to those in my small group during a time of need.

Signed: _____

Date: _____

GROUP MEMBERS

_____

_____

_____

_____

_____

_____

_____

_____

_____

_____

_____

Personal Devotion Time

Then God said, "Take your son, your only son, Isaac, whom you love, and go to the region of Moriah. Sacrifice him there as a burnt offering on one of the mountains I will tell you about" (Gen. 22:2).

Scripture Reading: Genesis 22:1-19

Isn't today's Scripture disturbing? We know that "from everyone who has been given much, much will be demanded" (Luke 12:48), but we'll gladly step aside and allow another to be called faithful if this is the kind of sacrifice required. However, we can't step aside quite as far as we would like. We have more in common with Abram, "the father of a multitude of nations" (Gen. 17:5, NASB), than we might think. Consider a few comparisons.

First, our most profound tests involve those dearest to us. You know it's true; you've been there. Each of us can remember a time when God called on us to surrender our hold over someone we loved—perhaps even someone we nearly worshiped.

What was Abraham's test?

_____

Have you ever experienced a test that involved someone dear to you?
❏ yes ❏ no

What was the test?

_____

How did you respond?

_____

Second, we also experience times when we believe we have received two seemingly opposite messages from God.

Abram understood God to say he would have more offspring than the number of stars in the sky. Then he received the command to sacrifice his only legitimate heir. As we continually trust the One who called us, we will eventually recognize that God truly is Reconciler of the utterly irreconcilable.

You see, God didn't mislead Abram. He told him to sacrifice his son on the altar and, most assuredly, Abram did. He did not slay his son; instead, he was able to offer God a living sacrifice.

Mind you, living sacrifices are not always easy to offer either. Sometimes releasing our grip on the person who remains with us can be a more painful test than releasing our grip on the person taken from our reach. We're presented with an ongoing test during which we must continually offer our precious ones to the One who loves them most.

Have you ever experienced a time when you felt you received two different messages from God?
❏ yes ❏ no

What were the messages, and how did you respond to them?

_____

Did God reconcile for you what seemed irreconcilable? If so, how?

_____

_____

I see a final comparison. God used Abraham and Isaac to teach others about Himself. The substitutionary offering of the ram caught by its horns in the thicket became one of the Bible's key images to convey the gospel message. The shadow of the cross fell on Mount Moriah that day. We all have been tied to the altar of death and then presented a chance to be loosed for eternal life by the perfect Lamb, One whose head was torn by thorns and was willing to take our place.

Define a "living sacrifice."

_____

Have you ever offered a living sacrifice?
❏ yes ❏ no

What did you learn about trusting God through the experience?

_____

_____

_____

Our present challenges may not be as dramatic as Abram's, but we, too, can allow our lives to become visual aids through which God teaches others about Himself—and His faithful ways. Read the poem God gave me during a time when He led me to my own Mount Moriah. Only you know how this message applies to you. Allow God to speak to your heart.

Trust Me with Your Isaac

For every Abraham who dares
to kiss the foreign field
where glory for a moment grasped
Is for a lifetime tilled . . .

The voice of God
speaks not but once
but 'til the traveler hears
"Abraham! Abraham! Bring your
Isaac here!"

"Bring not the blemished sacrifice.
What lovest thou the most?
Look not into the distance,
you'll find your Isaac close."

"I hear the tearing of your heart
torn between two loves,
the one your vision can behold
the Other hid above."

"Do you trust me, Abraham
with your gravest fear?
Will you pry your fingers loose
and bring your Isaac here?"

"Have I not made you promises?
Hold them tight instead!
I am the Lover of your soul—
the Lifter of your head."

"Believe me, O my Abraham
when blinded by the cost.
Arrange the wooded altar
and count your gains but loss."

"Let tears wash clean your blinded eyes
until unveiled you see—
the ram caught in the thicket there
to set your Isaac free."

"Perhaps I'll send him down the mount
to walk right by your side.
No longer in your iron grasp
but safer still in mine."

"Or I may wrap him in the wind
and sweep him from your sight
to better things beyond your reach—
believe with all your might!"

"Look up, beloved Abraham.
Can you count the stars?
Multitudes will stand to reap
from one dear friend of God."

"Pass the test, my faithful one;
bow to me as Lord.
Trust me with your Isaac—
see,
I am your great Reward."

Devotion and poem adapted from Beth Moore's *Whispers of Hope* (Nashville: LifeWay Press, 1998), 114-15.

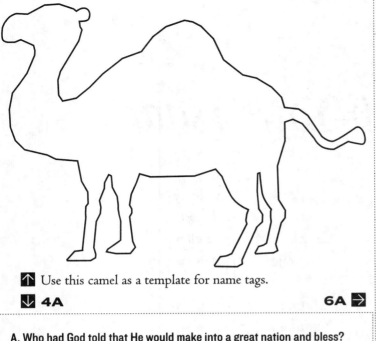

⬆ Use this camel as a template for name tags.

⬇ **4A**   **6A** ➡

A. Who had God told that He would make into a great nation and bless?

B. Who did Abraham want Isaac to marry?

C. What was one item the servant took with him as part of the bride price?

D. What sign did the servant request from God to know the woman God had for Isaac?

E. When did Rebekah appear on the scene?

F. How was Rebekah described?

G. Who is Laban?

H. How did the servant respond to God after Laban and Bethuel agreed to let Rebekah become Isaac's wife?

I. What request did Laban and Bethuel make?

J. What was Isaac doing when he looked up and saw the camels approaching?

K. What did Rebekah do when she learned the man in the distance was Isaac?

L. How long did Abraham walk with God?

M. Who buried Abraham?

N. Where was Abraham buried?

A. Where did Jacob first see Rachel?

B. Why wouldn't the men at the well water the sheep?

C. What did Jacob do when he saw Rachel?

D. Who was Laban?

E. What were the names of Laban's daughters?

F. Which daughter was described as having "weak eyes"?

G. How was Rachel described?

H. How long did Jacob agree to work for Rachel?

I. How did Laban deceive Jacob?

J. What was Laban's reasoning for his deception?

K. How long did Jacob end up working for Rachel?

L. Which sister was able to bear children first?

M. What was the name of Rachel's slave given to Jacob so that she could bear children?

N. How many children did Leah have?

O. What was the name of Rachel's child?

P. After Rachel gave birth to Joseph, what request did Jacob make of Laban?

Q. What had Laban learned about Jacob?

R. What wages did Jacob request from Laban?

S. What was the deal Jacob made with Laban?

T. How many days did Laban put between himself and Jacob?

Bonus points (5): Describe how Jacob separated the flocks.

Group One	Group Two	Group Three
Read Genesis 31:1-21 and answer the questions.	Read Genesis 31:22-44.	Read Genesis 31:44-55.
What was the conflict in these verses?	When did this occur?	What did Laban and Jacob do in these verses?
Who was involved?	What was the conflict?	How did they mark the place?
How was it resolved?	Who was involved?	What was the mound named?
What deceitful acts occurred?	What deceitful acts occurred?	How was the mound a witness?
How did God intervene?	How did God intervene?	

6B ⬆

Do you need to forgive or receive forgiveness from somone?

• What is getting in the way of your asking for forgiveness?

• What must you do in order to make amends?

• Write a prayer asking God to strengthen you to go to the person with whom you need to make amends.

7A ⬆

Group One	Group Two	Group Three
A 20-year-old young woman is date raped and becomes pregnant. What are some issues she must deal with? How can you as a believer minister to and support her?	A married woman walking across a parking lot at night is abducted and raped. What are some issues she must deal with? How can you as a believer minister to and support her?	A wife and mother of two is raped at gunpoint by a man who has broken into her home. What are some issues she must deal with? How can you as a believer minister to and support her?

7B ⬆

What do you find really stressful about your job whether
you are a stay at home mom or work for someone else?

_____ difficult boss

_____ an anti-Christian environment

_____ unrealistic expectations

_____ irritating coworkers

_____ other: _____

How can you relate most to Joseph's life?

_____ when he was thrown in the pit

_____ when he didn't know where he was going

_____ when he was blessed with success

_____ when he was falsely accused

_____ when he was thrown in prison

_____ when he made the most of his situation

What is your greatest motivation to live a pure and holy life?

_____ my love for God

_____ my desire to be obedient

_____ my fear of God—afraid I'll be punished if I don't

_____ God's love for me—I want to please Him

How have you experienced the Lord "with you" in times
of difficulty as well as success?

Describe a time when you felt forgotten by God
or someone else.

How might this story help remind you that God
is always there?

Have you ever suffered from a situation which was not
your fault or when life seemed unfair?

How did God make it right? Are you still waiting for things
to be made right? How can you learn from Joseph?

Group One

___ Joseph called his brothers spies.

___ The brothers insisted that they were coming to buy food.

___ Jacob did not send Benjamin.

___ Jacob sent 10 of his sons to buy grain in Egypt.

___ The brothers told Joseph they were 12 brothers, the youngest was with their father and
     one was no more.

___ Jacob learned there was grain in Egypt.

___ Joseph would not allow them to leave until the younger brother came back.

___ When Joseph's brothers arrived, Joseph recognized them but pretended to be a stranger.

Group Two

___ Joseph gave orders to fill their bags with grain, to put each man's silver in his sack, and to give
     them provisions for the journey.

___ Joseph became emotional when he heard his brothers talking about him.

___ They were to bring the younger brother back to Joseph so that their words could be verified.

___ Joseph had Simeon taken from them and bound before their eyes.

___ Joseph put them all in custody for three days.

___ The brothers loaded their grain and left.

___ When they stopped for the night, one of them opened his sack to get feed for his donkey and
     saw his silver in the sack.

___ The brothers thought they were being punished for Joseph's supposed death.

___ Joseph told them to leave one brother in prison and take the grain back to their homes.

___ The brothers became afraid that God was punishing them.

Group Three

___ Jacob refused to let Benjamin go.

___ The brothers reported that in order to trade in the land, they were to bring their youngest
     brother back.

___ The brothers arrived home and told Jacob all that had happened.

___ Reuben tried to get his father to consent by saying that he would be in charge and would
     make sure that Benjamin returned.

___ Jacob was angry because he felt as though they had deprived him of his children.

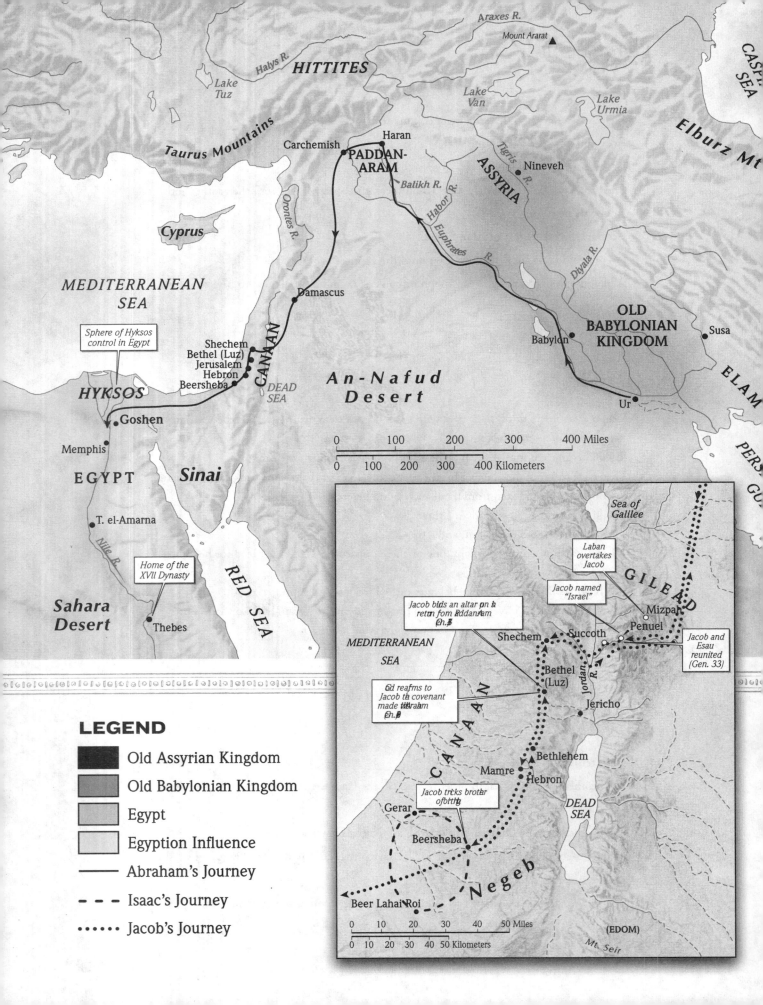

Araxes R.

Mount Ararat ▲

CASPIAN SEA

Halys R.

HITTITES

Lake Tuz

Taurus Mountains

Lake Van

Lake Urmia

Elburz Mt

Carchemish

Haran

PADDAN-ARAM

Balikh R.

Habor R.

ASSYRIA

Nineveh

Tigris R.

Orontes R.

Cyprus

MEDITERRANEAN SEA

Damascus

CANAAN

Euphrates R.

Diyala R.

OLD BABYLONIAN KINGDOM

Susa

Sphere of Hyksos control in Egypt

Shechem
Bethel (Luz)
Jerusalem
Hebron
Beersheba

DEAD SEA

An-Nafud Desert

Babylon

ELAM

HYKSOS

Goshen

Ur

PERSIAN GULF

Memphis

EGYPT

Sinai

0   100   200   300   400 Miles

0   100 200 300 400 Kilometers

T. el-Amarna

Nile R.

Home of the XVII Dynasty

RED SEA

Sahara Desert

Thebes

Sea of Galilee

Laban overtakes Jacob

GILEAD

Jacob named "Israel"

Mizpah

Jacob builds an altar on his return from Paddan-Aram (Ch.35)

Succoth

Penuel

Jacob and Esau reunited (Gen. 33)

MEDITERRANEAN SEA

Shechem

CANAAN

Bethel (Luz)

Jordan R.

God reaffirms to Jacob the covenant made with Abraham (Ch.35)

Jericho

Bethlehem

Mamre

Hebron

DEAD SEA

Jacob tricks brother of birthright

Gerar

Beersheba

Negeb

Beer Lahai Roi

(EDOM)

Mt. Seir

0   10   20   30   40   50 Miles

0 10 20 30 40 50 Kilometers

LEGEND

◼ Old Assyrian Kingdom

◼ Old Babylonian Kingdom

◼ Egypt

◻ Egyption Influence

—— Abraham's Journey

--- Isaac's Journey

••• Jacob's Journey